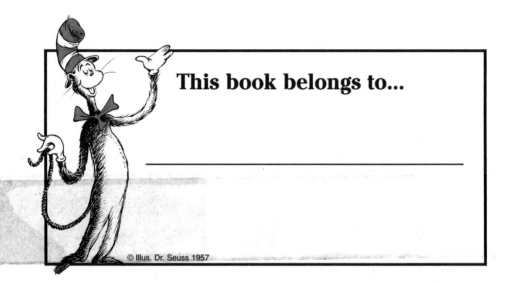

This book belongs to...

© Illus. Dr. Seuss 1957

Dr. Seuss's real name was Theodor Geisel.
On books he wrote to be illustrated by others,
he used the name Theo. LeSieg,
which is Geisel spelled backward.

Originally published in a different form by Random House, Inc., New York, and in
Canada by Random House of Canada Limited, Toronto ISBN 0-375-81039-0 (trade) -
ISBN 0-375-91039-5 (lib. bdg.).

BRIGHT AND EARLY BOOKS and colophon and RANDOM HOUSE and colophon are registered
trademarks of Random House, Inc.

SCHOLASTIC and associated logos are trademarks and/or registered trademarks of
Scholastic Inc.

This BOOK CLUB EDITION published by Scholastic Inc., 90 Old Sherman Turnpike, Danbury,
Connecticut 06816.

SPAM is a registered trademark of Geo. A. Hormel & Co.

ISBN 0-7172-6750-4

Printed in the U.S.A.

First Scholastic printing, December 2002

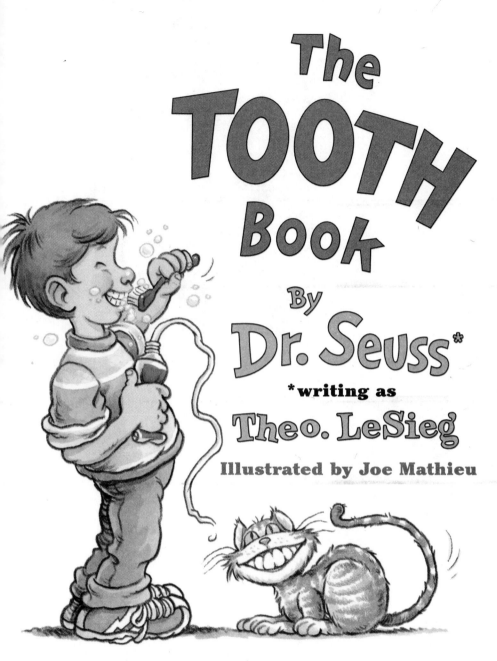

The TOOTH Book

By Dr. Seuss*

*writing as
Theo. LeSieg

Illustrated by Joe Mathieu

A Bright and Early Book
From BEGINNER BOOKS

A Division of Random House, Inc.

SCHOLASTIC Book Club Edition

Who has teeth?

Well . . .
look around
and you'll find out who.
You'll find
that red-headed uncles do.

Policemen do.
And zebras too.

And unicycle riders do.

And camels
and their drivers do!

Even little girls named Ruthie
all have teeth.
All Ruths are toothy.

Teeth!
You find them everywhere!
On mountaintops!
And in the air!

And if you care
to poke around,
you'll even find them
underground.

You'll find them
east, west, north, and south.
You'll find them
in a lion's mouth.

TEETH!
They are very much in style.

They must be
very much
worthwhile!

"They come in handy
when you chew,"
says Mr. Donald Driscoll Drew.

"That's why
my family
grew a few."

"They come in handy when you smile," says Smiling Sam the crocodile.

"They come in handy
in my job,"
says high trapezer
Mike McCobb.

"If I should ever
lose a tooth,
I'd lose my wife.
And that's the truth."

"Teeth come in handy when you speak," says news broadcaster Quincy Queek.

"Without my teeth
   I'd talk like ducks,
   and only broadcast
   quacks and klucks."

"You're lucky
   that you have your teeth,"
says a sad, sad snail
named Simon Sneeth.

"I don't have one!
I can never smile
like Smiling Sam
the crocodile."

"Clams have no teeth,"
says Pam the clam.
"I cannot eat
hot dogs
or ham."

"No teeth at all,"
  says Pam the clam.
"I cannot eat
  roast leg of lamb.
  Or peanuts! Pizzas!
  Popcorn! SPAM!
  Not even huckleberry jam!"

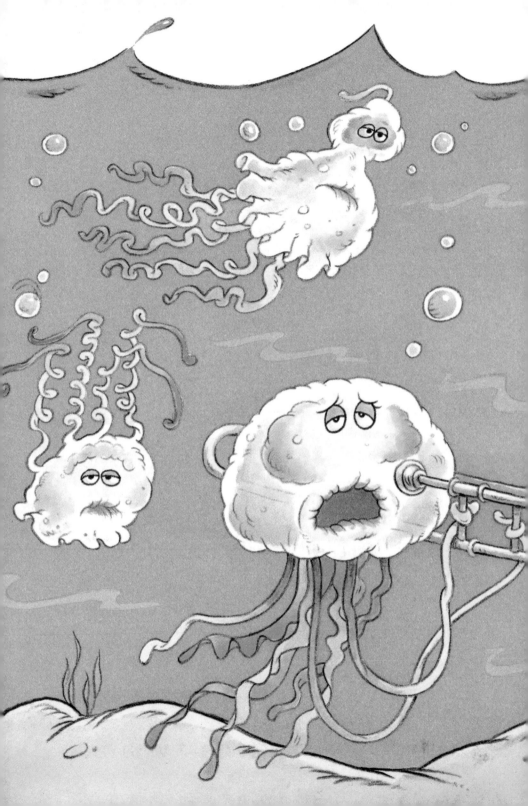

"Without teeth
we can't play trombones,"
says a jellyfish
named Jimbo Jones.

"I have no teeth," says Hilda Hen. "But women do. And so do men."

"So I have happy
news for you.
You will grow two sets!
Set one. Set two."

"You will lose
set number one.
And when you do,
it's not much fun.

"But then you'll grow
set number two!
32 teeth, and all brand-new.
16 downstairs, and 16 more
upstairs on the upper floor.

"And when you get
your second set,
THAT'S ALL THE TEETH
YOU'LL EVER GET!"

Don't gobble junk
like Billy Billings.
They say his teeth
have fifty fillings!

They sure are handy
when you smile.
So keep your teeth
around awhile.

And <u>never</u> bite your dentist
when he works inside your head.
Your dentist is
your teeth's best friend.

Bite carrot sticks instead!

DR. SEUSS (who was known as Theodor Geisel when he wasn't writing or drawing) wrote and illustrated 44 books for children and their lucky parents. But sometimes Dr. Seuss liked to write books and have someone else draw the pictures. For those books he used the pen name Theo. LeSieg (which is Geisel spelled backward!).